United States
Department of
Agriculture

Forest
Service

North Central
Research
Station

General Technical
Report **NC-262**

Ninth Workshop on Seedling Physiology and Growth Problems in Oak Plantings (Abstracts)

D.R. Weigel, J.W. Van Sambeek, and C.H. Michler

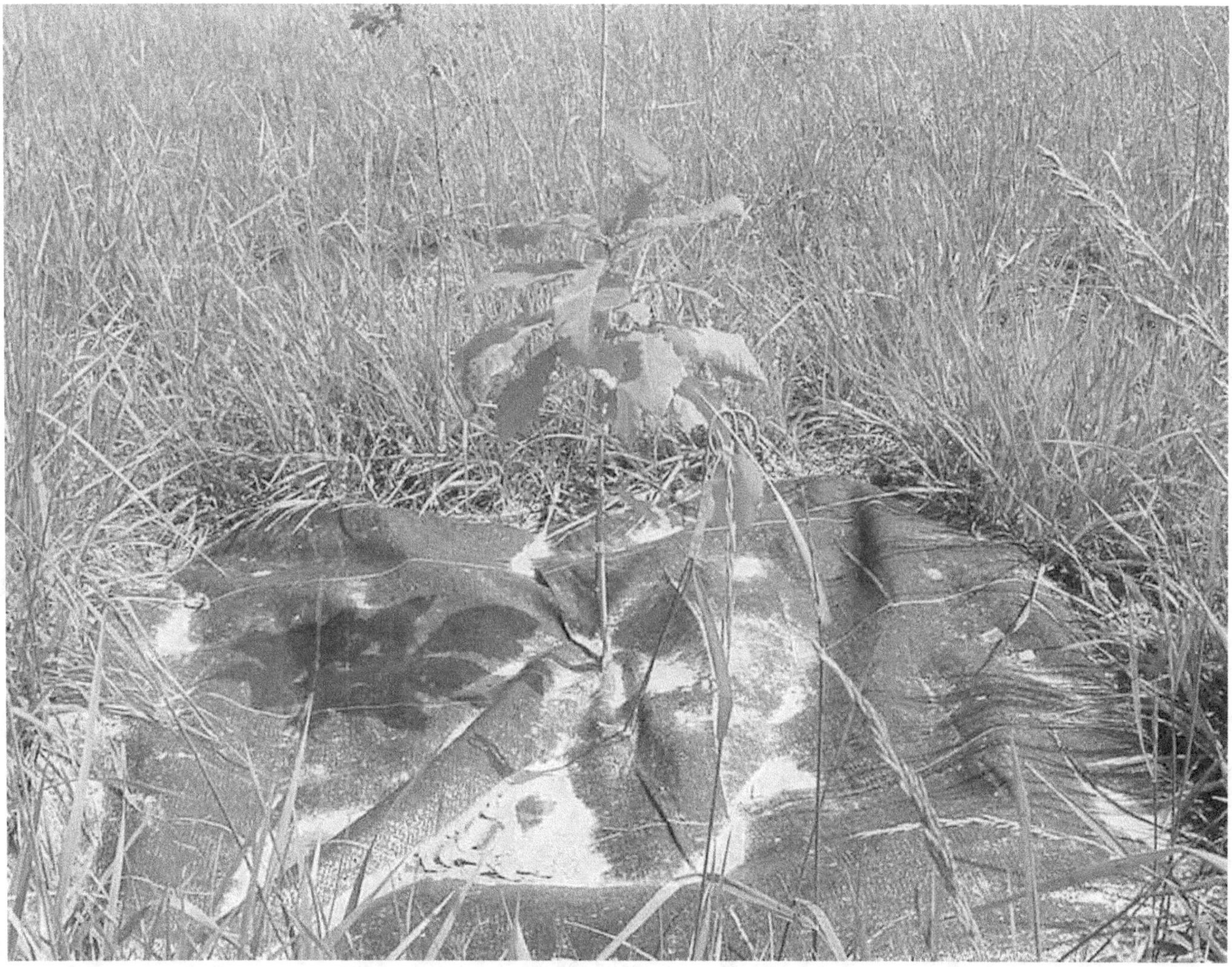

North Central Research Station
Forest Service-U.S. Department of Agriculture
1992 Folwell Avenue
St. Paul, Minnesota 55108
2005

NINTH WORKSHOP ON
SEEDLING PHYSIOLOGY AND GROWTH PROBLEMS IN OAK PLANTINGS
WEST LAFAYETTE, INDIANA, OCTOBER 18-20, 2004

Edited by

D.R. Weigel, J.W. Van Sambeek, and C.H. Michler

Sponsored by

USDA Forest Service, North Central Research Station
Department of Forestry and Natural Resources, Purdue University
Indiana Society of American Foresters

Held at

J.S. Wright Forestry Center
West Lafayette, Indiana

Published by

North Central Research Station
USDA Forest Service
St. Paul, Minnesota

ACKNOWLEDGMENTS

The authors wish to acknowledge the contributions of Liz Jackson and Beth Scharf who were in charge of registration. Thank you to Jim McKenna and Brian Beheler who helped arrange the field tours. We also thank the USDA Forest Service North Central Research Station, the Department of Forestry and Natural Resources at Purdue University, and the Indiana Society of American Foresters for sponsoring the workshop.

REVIEW PROCEDURE

Each abstract in this general technical report was critically reviewed by at least two editors. Revised abstracts were reviewed by each author and then submitted camera ready to North Central Research Station, USDA Forest Service, for publication. Individual authors are ultimately responsible for the accuracy of their papers.

DISCLAIMER

Mention of pesticides, fertilizer, equipment or trade names does not imply endorsement of these products or their applications by the USDA Forest Service.

TABLE OF CONTENTS

FLOOD TOLERANCE EVALUATION OF BOTTOMLAND OAKS IN A MULTI-CHANNEL FIELD LABORATORY

Mark V. Coggeshall
Center for Agroforestry, University of Missouri
Columbia, MO 65211-7270
J. W. Van Sambeek
USDA Forest Service, North Central Research Station
Columbia, MO 65211-7260
and
Scott E. Schlarbaum
Department of Forestry, Wildlife and Fisheries, University of Tennessee
Knoxville, TN 37996-4563

A multi-channel field laboratory was designed and constructed by the University of Missouri Center for Agroforestry at the Horticulture and Agroforestry Research Center to assess the flood tolerance of forages and hardwood seedlings. This facility located in the Missouri River floodplain consists of twelve 6-m wide x 180-m long channels that had minimal disturbance to the old-field riparian soils when soil from the retention pond was used to construct the berms. Each channel can be independently flooded for variable duration to specific depths with either flowing or stagnant water. For this study, we used nine channels arranged in a randomized complete block design of three blocks of three treatments each.

Treatments included five weeks of 15-cm-deep clear stagnant water, five weeks of 15-cm-deep turbid flowing water, and a non-flooded control. In mid-April 2003, we planted 1700 one-year-old, bareroot seedlings of cherrybark oak (*Quercus pagoda* Raf.), water oak (*Q. nigra* L.), willow oak (*Q. phellos* L.), and black walnut (*Juglans nigra* L.) from the University of Tennessee's Tree Improvement Program. Flood treatments were imposed 3 weeks later at the onset of seedling budbreak. Preplanting measurements included individual stem height, basal stem diameter, and number of first-order lateral roots. Ten-month post-planting measurements included survival, origin and length of the basal and apical new shoots, total number and length of new shoot growth, and amount of dieback on taproot.

Survival of all four species was greater in the non-flooded control channels than in either the flowing or stagnant water treatments. Because less than one percent of black walnut seedlings survived the flood treatments, walnut was not included in further analyses. There were no statistical differences in oak survival or growth between the flowing and stagnant water treatments. Willow oak had the best survival (81.4%) followed by cherrybark oak (66.7%), and then water oak (59.9%). Willow oak seedlings produced 3.7 new shoots (many of which were basal sprouts) with an average combined length of 71 cm. In contrast, water oak seedlings produced 2.9 new shoots with a combined length of 52 cm. Growth for both species exceeded that of cherrybark oak which produced 2.8 elongating shoots with a combined length of 19 cm. Approximately 15 percent of the surviving cherrybark oak seedlings exhibited greater than 50 percent dieback of the taproot compared to 21 percent of the willow oak and 26 percent of the water oak seedlings. From these data, we conclude planted willow oaks are more tolerant to prolonged spring flood events at the onset of spring budbreak than are planted seedlings of water oak or cherrybark oak, all of which are more tolerant of flooding than planted black walnut seedlings.

PERFORMANCE OF NORTHERN RED OAK SEEDLINGS ACROSS A PH GRADIENT

Anthony S. Davis and **Douglass F. Jacobs**
Hardwood Tree Improvement and Regeneration Center
Department of Forestry and Natural Resources, Purdue University
West Lafayette, IN 47907

Northern red oak (*Quercus rubra* L.) seedlings were grown from acorns in 4-gallon containers in a greenhouse. Growing medium was amended to a pH of 3.50, 4.25, 5.00, and 5.75 using tri-weekly applications of aluminum sulfate. In addition, seedlings were subjected to either: (1) addition of a 16- to 18-month controlled-release fertilizer (CRF), (2) mycorrhizal inoculation, (3) the combination of CRF and mycorrhizal inoculation, or (4) a control with neither CRF or mycorrhizal inoculation of the growing medium.

Mycorrhizal inoculation did not influence seedling root or shoot growth or foliar nutrient status. Addition of CRF to the growing medium increased the number of leaves, seedling leaf area, and leaf dry weight, as well as foliar N and P content. Seedlings grown in the CRF-amended medium had more first-order lateral roots than seedlings that did not receive CRF. Growing medium pH influenced seedling height, root-collar diameter, foliar N and P concentration and content, and all leaf morphological parameters.

The results of this study indicate that northern red oak may be able to successfully establish under more acidic conditions than had previously been identified. The addition of CRF to the growing media of containerized seedlings could be designed to maintain seedling nutrient levels at an adequate level into the second growing season. The addition of CRF could benefit seedling establishment when outplanting occurs on nutrient-poor sites where the nursery cultural regime could be adjusted for site-specific nutrient deficiencies.

EVALUATION OF RPM™ OAK SEEDLINGS IN AFFORESTING FLOODPLAIN CROP FIELDS ALONG THE MISSOURI RIVER

Daniel C. Dey and **John M. Kabrick**
USDA Forest Service, North Central Research Station
Columbia, MO 65211-7260
and
Michael A. Gold
Center for Agroforestry, University of Missouri
Columbia, MO 65211-7260

Regenerating oaks in agricultural floodplains is problematic because of their slow juvenile shoot growth, intense plant competition, seasonal flooding, and browsing by wildlife. Planting large nursery stock has been recommended to increase the competitiveness of oak seedlings. The Forrest Keeling Nursery in Missouri developed the Root Production Method (RPM™) using air root pruning techniques to produce large seedlings with dense, fibrous root systems in 3- or 5-gallon containers.

In crop fields along the lower Missouri River, we are evaluating RPM™ seedlings of pin oak (*Quercus palustris* Muenchh.) and swamp white oak (*Q. bicolor* Willd.) and comparing them to 1-0 bareroot seedlings of both species. The RPM™ oak planting stock is substantially larger than the 1-0 bareroot oak seedlings, regardless of species. For example, one-year-old pin oak RPM™ seedlings grown in 3-gallon containers averaged 236 cm^3 in root volume, 117 g in root dry weight, 21 mm in basal stem diameter, and 235 cm in shoot length; whereas 1-0 pin oak bareroot seedlings had an average root volume of 26 cm^3, root dry weight of 17 g, basal stem diameter of 7.6 mm, and shoot length of 70 cm. We are also assessing the benefits of planting oaks in bedded soils with a grass cover crop.

After three years, basal diameter increment and survival were greater (P < 0.01) for RPM™ seedlings than for the bareroot stock. There was no difference in performance between the 3- and 5-gallon RPM™ seedlings. Survival of RPM™ seedlings was higher (94%) than that of bareroot swamp white oak (76%) or bareroot pin oak seedlings (54%). Cover crop and soil mounding has had no effect on oak seedling survival or growth. Many of RPM™ trees have resprouted and have lost more height during the first three years than the bareroot seedlings primarily in response to cottontail rabbit herbivory. Stem girdling has been greater on oaks in the natural vegetation than oaks in the redtop grass cover crop. Rabbits can be discouraged from damaging oaks by maintaining a low vegetative cover in winter. Swamp white oak RPM™ seedlings produced acorns annually the first four years. The number of oaks producing acorns and production per tree increased over the four years. Results to date indicate that planting large RPM™ seedlings in a cover crop of redtop grass can improve early oak regeneration success.

RESPONSE OF WHITE OAK AND BLACK OAK SEEDLINGS TO A MID-STORY REMOVAL

Dylan N. Dillaway and **Jeff Stringer**
Department of Forestry, University of Kentucky
Lexington, KY 40546-0073

White oak (*Quercus alba* L.) and black oak (*Quercus velutina* Lam.) often dominate stands on intermediate to high quality sites. In these stands there is often a bank of advanced oak regeneration (>1 ft. tall) in place. However, this advanced oak regeneration rarely achieves a co-dominant or dominant status when a regeneration harvest is performed. A mid-story removal has been shown to increase the vigor of oak seedlings, but has not been widely tested. The length of suppression could affect the ability of oak seedlings to respond vigorously when provided with additional light. Seedlings on the forest floor can range from one to >20 years old with minimal height growth. Root ages of these seedlings can be far older than the stem of the seedlings. This study will assess the response of suppressed white oak and black oak seedlings to a mid-story removal.

To obtain information on the above and belowground attributes of the seedling population, 120 white oak seedlings were selected from four stands and destructively sampled. Root age was determined 1 cm below the root collar. The mean stem and root age was 7 years old for true seedlings. The mean stem and root age of seedling sprouts were 6 and 9 years old, respectively. In many stands there are very few true seedlings. Seedling stems older than 10 years are very rare; however, it was not uncommon to find a seedling with a root system older than 10 years. Repeated sprouting could have an effect on the seedlings ability to respond when suitable conditions are created for rapid growth. This rapid growth is needed in order to out-compete co-occurring species.

This study will be used to analyze different age classes of seedlings in the advanced regeneration pool and first year seedlings resulting from planted acorns and 1-0 bareroot seedlings. In order to increase light levels at the forest floor, twenty percent of the basal area was removed from the stands. This study will allow us to assess the timing of treatments, the type (age) of seedlings needed, and the associated vigor of different types of seedlings upon release.

DEVELOPMENT OF NORTHERN RED OAK ROOTED CUTTING AND ENRICHMENT PLANTING SYSTEMS

Matthew H. Gocke, Jamie Schuler, Daniel J. Robison and **Barry Goldfarb**
Department of Forestry, North Carolina State University
Raleigh, NC 27695-8002

Enrichment planting may provide an efficient means to establish elite northern red oak (*Quercus rubra* L.) genotypes in recently harvested natural forests. However, planting northern red oak (NRO) seedlings into natural stands has proven difficult in the past, especially when competition and other stress factors are not controlled. Likewise, genetic improvement of oak for timber production has been limited due to relatively long periods of juvenility, episodic seed production, and slow growth resulting in long progeny testing times. Two areas of research have, therefore, been initiated by the North Carolina State University Hardwood Research Co-operative to identify successful enrichment planting techniques capable of deploying elite genotypes: 1) vegetative propagation techniques for NRO stem cuttings, and 2) establishment techniques for NRO seedlings within emerging natural regeneration. Developing successful techniques for both would allow for the substitution of seedlings with rooted cuttings. Though vegetative propagation of elite NRO individuals does not represent population genetic improvement (as in the case of a breeding program), it is an extremely efficient means to capture high quality genotypes and, through deployment, establish higher quality - faster growing trees. Such an approach can be readily linked to existing genetic improvement programs as well.

Of several successful vegetative propagation techniques reported in the literature, rooting juvenile softwood stem cuttings that are collected from pruned stock plants under conditions of high humidity offer the greatest potential for producing a large number of high quality NRO reforestation stock. Adopting this strategy for coppice sprouts obtained from recently felled trees of high phenotypic value could further accelerate the deployment of elite NRO individuals. Because maturation, pruning location, rooting environment, collection time, and hormone treatment affect rooting success, we are continuing studies initiated in 2001 to develop an efficient rooted cutting production system. Attention has also been placed on post-rooting cultural practices for rooted cuttings and on pruning treatments of stock plants designed to optimize shoot production.

Enrichment planting trials have been established in the North Carolina mountains on recently harvested sites with natural regeneration emerging in clearcut and shelterwood systems. NRO 1-0 bareroot seedlings were planted in 2001 in two clearcuts and two shelterwood cuts using weed mats and glyphosate to control competition and pelletized fertilizers to enhance fertility. The plantings have been monitored yearly.

A successful post-harvest enrichment planting system would facilitate the enhancement of preferred species on sites with limited oak regeneration. It would also be an effective means to deploy vegetatively propagated elite genotypes without the use of challenging clean plantation culture.

EVALUATING DESICCATION SENSITIVITY OF NORTHERN RED OAK ACORNS
USING X-RAY IMAGE ANALYSIS

Rosa C. Goodman and **Douglass F. Jacobs**
Hardwood Tree Improvement and Regeneration Center
Department of Forestry and Natural Resources, Purdue University
West Lafayette, IN 47907

Desiccation of northern red oak (*Quercus rubra* L.) acorns can have a major influence on seed viability. Recalcitrant behavior of northern red oak acorns was studied to examine the effects of moisture content (MC) on germination and early growth. Because it is rapid and non-destructive, X-ray image analysis was chosen to assess cotyledon damage in acorns subjected to varying amounts of desiccation.

Half-sib acorns collected from five sources were desiccated to one of four target MC levels (30, 25, 20, or 15%) or maintained as non-desiccated controls (35 to 38%). Each acorn was X-rayed before and after drying to respective MC treatments and sown into individual containers in a greenhouse. Germinated seedlings were evaluated for number of days needed to reach the developmental stages of radicle emergence, epicotyl emergence, and full emergence of the first leaf flush. Height and root-collar diameter were measured and number of leaf flushes was recorded 80 days after sowing. X-ray images were scored qualitatively for each acorn according to the degree of cotyledon-cotyledon and cotyledon-pericarp separation.

Family and MC had a significant influence on all variables. The percent of each sample to reach each stage, height, and root collar diameter declined with decreasing MC and dropped most notably between 20 and 15 percent MC. X-ray image separation scores for both cotyledon-cotyledon and cotyledon-pericarp were more closely correlated to the percent of each sample to reach each of the three developmental stages than MC level. These findings demonstrate the potential of X-ray image analysis to provide a rapid and nondestructive means for successfully predicting acorn viability.

TRANSPLANT SHOCK OF NORTHERN RED OAK SEEDLINGS FOLLOWING SIMULATED DROUGHT AS INFLUENCED BY ROOT MORPHOLOGY

Douglass F. Jacobs, Francis Salifu, and **Anthony Davis**
Hardwood Tree Improvement and Regeneration Center
Department of Forestry and Natural Resources, Purdue University
West Lafayette, IN 47907

Transplant shock, implicated by depressed seedling physiological response associated with moisture or nutrient stress immediately following planting, limits early plantation establishment. We investigated the impacts of simulated drought and transplant root volume on predawn leaf xylem water potential, photosynthetic assimilation rates, stomatal conductance, and growth of northern red oak (*Quercus rubra* L.) seedlings to explain susceptibility of these plants to transplant shock.

Bareroot oak seedlings were graded into four root volume categories, planted, and then kept well watered or subjected to moisture stress. To simulate drought, irrigation was discontinued for 22 days (low moisture stress), 44 days, 66 days, and 88 days (high moisture stress) after which all seedlings were re-watered to examine drought recovery.

Transplant shock was implicated by restricted shoot growth, lower predawn leaf xylem water potentials, and depressed photosynthetic assimilation rates. These changes increased with increasing transplant root volume. Simulated drought lowered the predawn xylem water potentials to -2.5 MPa in high moisture stress plants while xylem water potentials never fell below -0.7 MPa in well watered seedlings. Transpiration rate, photosynthetic assimilation rate, stomatal conductance, and seedling growth decreased with increasing moisture stress. Unlike seedlings exposed to 22 and 44 days of stimulated drought, seedlings exposed to 66 or 88 days of simulated drought never fully recovered when re-watered. The most effective drought avoidance mechanisms were root growth, stomatal regulation, reduced leaf area, and higher growth allocation to roots relative to shoots.

PLANTED OAKS AND NATURAL INVASION IN BOTTOMLAND HARDWOOD FORESTS OF THE LOWER MISSISSIPPI ALLUVIAL VALLEY

Bobby D. Keeland and **John W. McCoy**
USGS, National Wetlands Research Center
Lafayette, LA 70506
and
Kristi Wharton
USDA Forest Service, Southern Research Station
Pineville, LA 71360

Conversion of woodlands to other land-use types has resulted in the loss of over 80 percent of the historic bottomland hardwood forests of the Lower Mississippi Valley. This represents a loss of more than 6 million ha of forested wetlands. Heightened interests in reforestation and the mixed results associated with past afforestation efforts emphasize the need for more and better information on successful tree planting and the effects of natural woody invasion.

We studied the survival and growth of 9- to 12-year-old planted oak seedlings and natural invasion by other woody species in 459 plots on 18 fields in Arkansas, Louisiana, and Mississippi. To assess the natural woody invasion, 200 m² plots were established at 50 m intervals from forested edges. We encountered six species of planted oaks, more than 19 species of potential overstory invaders, and 13 small tree or shrub species. Survival of both planted oaks and natural woody invaders was uneven among locations. We found as few as 25 and as many as 898 oaks and between 170 and 11,095 natural invaders per hectare.

Natural woody invaders outnumbered planted oaks at all but two locations and were most abundant when the plots were within 450 m of a forest edge. The majority of light seeded invaders were found within 200 m of the forest edge. Green ash (*Fraxinus pennsylvanica* Marsh.), Pumpkin ash (*F. profunda* (Bush) Bush), sweetgum (*Liquidambar styraciflua* L.), American elm (*Ulmus americana* L.), and cedar elm (*U. crassifolia* Nutt.) made up 49 percent of all invaders and were found on greater than 50 percent of all plots. We found multiple factors affected seedling survival included soils, topographic position, rainfall, and herbivory.

IS SEEDLING GRADING BENEFICIAL TO ARTIFICIAL REGENERATION OF NORTHERN RED OAKS?

Paul P. Kormanik and **Shi-Jean S. Sung**
USDA Forest Service, Southern Research Station
Athens, GA 30602
and
Stanley J. Zarnoch
USDA Forest Service, Southern Research Station
Asheville, NC 28802

Effective and consistent success with artificial regeneration of northern red oak (*Quercus rubra* L.) has been achieved on many sites using 1-0 graded seedlings produced with the nursery protocol developed by the USDA Forest Service at the Institute of Tree Root Biology in cooperation with the Georgia Forestry Commission. Small northern red oak (NRO) plantings of one or two acres have demonstrated that artificial regeneration can play a vital role in restoring this species in stands where it has been difficult to establish NRO naturally for different reasons.

In preliminary testing, the minimum standards normally used for evaluating NRO for outplanting in our regeneration protocol have included first-order lateral roots (FOLR), heights, and root collar diameters of 6, 70 cm, and 8 mm, respectively. For over a decade, research with over a hundred different half-sib oak seedlots have indicated that 20 to 30 percent of the seedlings from any given seedlot do not meet these minimum standards and thus are subsequently culled upon lifting. Some questions have been raised as to the culling standards used since it is not unusual to cull a third of the seedlings from each seedlot. Although they did not meet height and root collar diameter standards, we have tested some seedlings with higher FOLR numbers than the minimum FOLR standard. In addition, several studies have shown seedlings under shade can rapidly shed lateral roots and lose benefits of FOLR grading.

It has been difficult to test the range of grading standards because herbicide usage has been so restrictive on National Forest lands and mechanical release is difficult and costly to implement. In 2000 a small area became available for grading standard testing on the Tusquitee Ranger District on the Nantahala National Forest in North Carolina. Acorns from five NRO half-sib seedlots obtained from the Watuga seed orchard in Tennessee were used in this study. Seedlings were grown according to our nursery protocol and root pruned to a standard length of 15 cm for the FOLR and 30 cm for the taproot. The 1-0 seedlings were classified as small, medium, and large based primarily on number of FOLR. The range in FOLRs for each group was 0 to 6, 7 to 13, and 14 to 22, respectively. The fourth year mean survival for small, medium, and large seedlings was 22, 67, and 77 percent, respectively. Mean fourth year height and diameter at breast height for small, medium, and large seedlings were 138 cm and 4 mm, 190 cm and 9 mm, and 199 cm and 10 mm, respectively. Whether seedling grading is beneficial depends highly on what the nursery does and planting conditions.

UNDERPLANTING PIN OAK SEEDLINGS IN BOTTOMLAND FORESTS MANAGED AS GREENTREE RESERVOIRS

Nicholas Krekeler
St. Charles County Parks Department
St. Charles, MO 63301
John M. Kabrick and **Daniel C. Dey**
USDA Forest Service North Central Research Station
Columbia, MO 65211
and
Michael Wallendorf
Missouri Department of Conservation
Columbia, MO 65201

Underplanting bottomland oaks may be necessary to maintain them in future stands where advanced reproduction is lacking. In bottomland forests of the Mingo Basin in southeastern Missouri, we compared the survival of underplanted pin oak (*Quercus palustris* Muenchh.) acorns, bareroot seedlings, and RPM™ container-grown seedlings in stands where the mid-story was thinned with and without controlling the ground flora with herbicide.

We used a randomized complete-block design replicated three times in declining bottomland oak stands and three times in healthy bottomland oak stands at Duck Creek Conservation Area and Mingo National Wildlife Refuge. Mid-story thinning decreased the canopy cover from 90 percent to 83 percent. After one growing season, underplanted RPM™ container seedlings had the greatest survival (87 percent without and 77 percent with ground flora control) followed by bareroot seedlings (86 percent without and 66 percent with ground flora control). The survival of both bareroot and container-grown seedlings increased with increasing initial seedling height and decreasing canopy cover. Direct-seeded acorns had the poorest survival (9 percent without and 4 percent with ground flora control). For surviving trees, bareroot seedlings had lower ($P < 0.001$) height growth rate than natural seedlings, direct-seeded stock, and RPM™ container-grown stock. However height growth for all stock was fair and ranged from 0.35 feet (bareroot) to 0.65 feet (RPM™) and both bareroot and RPM™ stock were > 2 feet tall at the end of the first growing season. Controlling competing ground flora with herbicide did not increase seedling growth regardless of stock type.

Based on these early results, container-grown stock performed the best but bareroot seedlings appeared nearly equally suitable for underplanting in bottomland forests. Ground flora control substantially decreased survival and did not improve seedling growth sufficiently to warrant its use. We will continue to monitor these seedlings to determine their competitive capacity for regenerating these stands.

COMPARATIVE DEVELOPMENT OF PLANTED CHERRYBARK OAK-SWEETGUM MIXTURES: IMPLICATIONS FOR FUTURE MIXED-SPECIES PLANTINGS IN THE LOWER MISSISSIPPI ALLUVIAL VALLEY

Brian R. Lockhart
USDA Forest Service, Southern Research Station
Center for Bottomland Hardwoods Research
Stoneville, MS 38776
Andrew W. Ezell and **John D. Hodges**
Department of Forestry, College of Forest Resources, Mississippi State University
Mississippi State, MS 39763
and
Wayne K. Clatterbuck
Department of Forestry, Wildlife & Fisheries, University of Tennessee
Knoxville, TN 37996-4563

Planting oaks in abandoned agricultural fields and pastures in the Lower Mississippi Alluvial Valley has received much attention in the past 20 years. A common afforestation prescription is to plant oaks on a 12- x 12-ft spacing. Recently, concern has been expressed about planting 302 oaks per acre and the resulting effects of early intra-specific competition following canopy closure. Recommendations have included planting a greater number of species in intimate mixtures, but little is known about how such stands will develop.

A mixed-species case study was installed in Oktibbeha County, MS in 1982 and involved intimate mixtures of cherrybark oak (*Quercus pagoda* Raf.) and sweetgum (*Liquidambar styraciflua* L.). Spacing arrangements included 8- x 8-ft and 5- x 5-ft spacings where a row of alternating cherrybark oak and sweetgum seedlings was surrounded on both sides with rows of pure sweetgum. An additional spacing arrangement involved two pure rows of sweetgum on each side of an alternating row of cherrybark oak and sweetgum in a 5- x 5-ft spacing. Height and diameter-at-breast-height (d.b h.) were measured following the 8th, 10th, 17th, and 21st growing seasons.

Sweetgum was taller in height and larger in d.b.h. than cherrybark oak early in plantation development. By the 17th growing season, cherrybark oak was similar in height and d.b.h. with sweetgum and by the 21st growing season was taller in height and larger in d.b.h. than sweetgum in two of the three spacing arrangements.

The ascendance of cherrybark oak above sweetgum in an intimate plantation mixture follows documented natural cherrybark oak-sweetgum development patterns. Afforestation objectives in the Lower Mississippi Alluvial Valley that involve mixed species plantings must be based on known stand development patterns.

A COMPARISON OF SITE PREPARATION AND SOWING TECHNIQUES FOR DIRECT SEEDING BOTTOMLAND RED OAKS IN THE LOWER MISSISSIPPI ALLUVIAL VALLEY

Brian R. Lockhart
USDA Forest Service Southern Research Station
Center for Bottomland Hardwoods Research
Stoneville, MS 38776
Bob Keeland and **John McCoy**
USGS National Wetlands Research Center
Lafayette, LA 70506
and
Thomas J. Dean
School of Renewable Natural Resources, Louisiana State University
Baton Rouge, LA 70803

Prior to European settlement, bottomland hardwood forests covered about 24 million acres in the Lower Mississippi Alluvial Valley (LMAV). Due to the rich nature of these alluvial soils and the development of flood control structures, much of this land has been converted to agricultural production. Conversion of nearly 500,000 acres of agricultural land back to forest has occurred, due primarily to the advent of government cost-share programs such as the Conservation Reserve and Wetlands Reserve Programs. Unfortunately, many difficulties have been reported in afforesting these former agricultural fields, chief among these has been poor survival of sowed acorns and planted oak seedlings. Therefore, a study was initiated to compare different intensities of site preparation and acorn sowing methods for afforesting previously farmed bottomland hardwood sites in the LMAV.

Acorns of water oak (*Quercus. nigra* L.), willow oak (*Q. phellos* L.), and Nuttall oak (*Q. nuttallii* Palmer) were planted on two wildlife management areas and two national wildlife refuges in eastern Louisiana. Six site preparation treatments, implemented on one-acre treatment plots, included no discing, strip discing, single discing before and then after sowing, and double discing before sowing. A rolling treatment was added to additional single disc and double disc treatments. Two sowing methods, one employing a Max-merge seed drill and the other a Cyclone broadcast spreader, were used to plant the acorns during the fall of 1993 and spring of 1994. Two additional treatments, hand planting and machine planting of 1-0 bareroot oak seedlings, were included in each species and site combination.

Six years after establishment, few consistent differences were found in oak density between sowing methods (seed drill versus broadcast seeding), fall sowing versus spring sowing, and sowing acorns versus planting oak seedlings. Results indicated that some degree of site preparation is needed to establish oak seedlings as the greatest number of seedlings per acre were found on the single disc and double disc treatments. Nuttall oak had greater densities than either water oak or willow oak on sites where multiple oak species were planted while water oak showed its best results with Cyclone broadcast seeding. There was a trend for the rolling treatment to increase number of oak seedlings on disced plots. These results indicate that no one prescription for oak regeneration fits all potential afforestation projects in the LMAV.

EFFECTS OF FIRE AND THINNING ON OAK AND OTHER HARDWOOD SPECIES REGENERATION IN MIXED OAK FORESTS OF SOUTHEASTERN OHIO

Brian C. McCarthy and **Matthew A. Albrecht**
Department of Environmental and Plant Biology, Ohio University
Athens, OH 45701

We conducted a study of hardwood regeneration in the mixed oak forests of unglaciated southeastern Ohio following various silvicultural practices. Our study was conducted at three separate forests within the region.

Each forest contained a control stand and three treatment stands. The treatments included prescribed fire, thinning, and thinning followed by prescribed fire. Thinnings were conducted in the winter of 2000-2001 and prescribed fires were implemented in the spring of 2001. Within each treatment unit (12 total) we placed ten 20- x 50-m vegetation plots (120 total), stratified by an integrated moisture index. Within each 20- x 50-m plot, we designated three 10- x 10-m sub-plots as regeneration plots (360 total), and recorded height on all woody stems < 10 cm diameter at breast height (d.b.h.). Woody regeneration was sampled prior to treatment (summer 2000) and immediately following treatments (summer 2001).

Seedlings responded as a function of size class. Small seedling (< 10 cm tall) density increased dramatically following treatments that utilized prescribed fire. Seedling densities in the medium size class (10 to 50 cm tall) were unresponsive to treatments. Stem densities in the large seedling size class (50 to 140 cm tall) increased ($P < 0.05$) in the thinning treatments. Likewise, saplings responded differentially by size class. The smallest saplings (140 cm ht to 2.5 cm d.b h.) decreased as a result of prescribed fires while the largest saplings (6.0 to 10.0 cm d.b h.) were not reduced.

Prescribed fire was effective at reducing mesophytic competitors (e.g., *Acer* spp.) with oak (*Quercus* spp.). However, oak seedlings and saplings did not respond to the treatments within the first post-fire growing season. Prescribed fire, but not thinning, resulted in a decline in both the seedling stratum and sapling stratum in species richness and Shannon-Weiner diversity. Community composition differences were greatest in those treatments receiving prescribed fire.

In summary, we found treatments to cause heterogeneous community responses as a function of species, size class, and moisture availability. In the absence of additional treatments and time, the effect on oak regeneration is unclear.

REGENERATION CONCERNS IN AREAS IMPACTED BY SUDDEN OAK DEATH

Douglas D. McCreary
University of California Integrated Hardwood Range Management Program
Browns Valley, CA 95918

Sudden Oak Death (SOD) is a new disease affecting several oak (*Quercus* spp.) species in California. It is caused by *Phytophthora ramorum*, a fungus-like water mold that causes bark cankers that girdles and kills mature trees. To date, this disease has been reported on four of California's twenty species of native oaks. Three are members of the black oak subgenus; coast live oak (*Quercus agrifolia* Nee), California black oak (*Q. kelloggii* Newb.), and Shreve oak (*Q. parvula* v. shrevei): one is a member of the intermediate oak subgenus; canyon live oak (*Q. chrysolepis* Liebm.). To date, it does not appear that members of the white oak subgenus are susceptible. *P. ramorum* has also been confirmed on dozens of other species of plants, including tanoak (*Lithocarpus densiflora* (Hook. & Arn.) Rehd.), closely related to true oaks (also in the Fagacae family). There are also another thirty associated species that are believed to harbor the organism, but have not yet been officially confirmed as hosts.

In areas impacted by SOD, there is concern that invasive weeds could replace the dying vegetation. This concern is based on repeated observations that highly competitive exotic plants often invade and occupy sites that lose their existing tree and shrub communities. This usually occurs in the aftermath of catastrophic events such as wildfire, but is also a risk following loss due to insects or disease. In spite of the name, loss of trees and shrubs following SOD infection on forested sites is usually gradual, rather than sudden, complicating restoration strategies. In addition, there is currently little information available regarding genetic resistance of oaks, and a poor understanding of how susceptible oak seedlings are to the disease. At present, oak seedlings of the four confirmed host species do not display SOD symptoms and are thought not to harbor the disease organism. Yet this does not mean that these oak seedlings will not become infected as they grow older and larger.

This uncertainty has made land managers reluctant to replant susceptible oak species in areas suffering high levels of tree loss. Until more is known about the disease, including identifying genotypes that are resistant, it is unlikely landowners or managers will seriously undertake efforts to replants oaks in areas affected by sudden oak death.

TWENTY-YEAR PERFORMANCE IN A WHITE OAK PROVENANCE TEST

Philip A. O'Connor
IDNR Division of Forestry, Vallonia State Tree Nursery
Vallonia, IN 47281

In 1983 a limited-range provenance test for white oak (*Quercus alba* L.) was established at the Starve Hollow SRA in cooperation with the North Central Forest Experiment Station. The planting was made up of half-sib progeny of nine families/provenances representing six states from Mississippi through Minnesota. The provenances range from 34.4° through 45.0° north latitude, and the planting site at 38.5° is just south of the midpoint of that range.

Two-year-old seedlings were outplanted in six replications of four-tree family plots on an 8- x 8-ft spacing. Weed control was maintained through crown closure with herbicide. The planting was measured periodically, and thinned to the best two trees per plot after the 15th growing season. The most recent height and diameter-at-breast-height measurements were recorded following the 20th growing season when epicormic branching was also scored on a 1 (no epicormic branching) to 4 (very heavy epicormic branching) scale.

There was a strong negative correlation between latitude and both diameter and height (−0.91 and −0.89, respectively). The Mississippi provenance (34.4°), which remained cold hardy almost 300 miles north of its native range, ranked first for diameter growth at 8.13 inches d.b h. or 115 percent of the plantation mean. It ranked fourth for height growth at 47.3 feet or 105 percent of the plantation mean. An Indiana provenance (39.1°) ranked first for height and second for diameter at 49.7 feet and 8.05 inches respectively. At the other end of the range, the Minnesota provenance (45.0°) performed poorly at 70 percent of the mean for diameter and 83 percent of the mean for height.

Growth data by itself is impressive, but it only tells part of the story. Epicormic branching is an indicator of stress within the tree and is a serious defect from a timber perspective. Scoring for epicormic branching indicated the lowest rating (fewest sprouts) for trees planted close to their native range and the highest rating for trees planted the farthest from their native range (in either direction).

FIELD PERFORMANCE OF GRADED NORTHERN RED OAK SEEDLINGS PLANTED UNDER FOUR OVERSTORY TREATMENTS IN TENNESSEE: TWO-YEAR RESULTS

Christopher M. Oswalt and *Wayne K. Clatterbuck*
Department of Forestry, Wildlife and Fisheries, University of Tennessee
Knoxville, TN 37996-4563

Oak replacement persists as an obstacle to high quality hardwood management, especially on highly productive sites. Difficulties in naturally regenerating oak can be viewed as the result of social and economic constraints imposed by the biological solution, not the lack of a solution. As a result, economically viable alternatives are being explored to maintain oak as an important component of future stands including artificial regeneration; however, to be successful, studies are needed on artificial oak regeneration to enhance the methods and explore impediments.

We examined the growth of outplanted high-quality 1-0 northern red oak (*Quercus rubra* L.) seedlings after four overstory treatments on the Ames Plantation in west Tennessee. Sixty seedlings were outplanted within each of twelve two-acre treatment units, resulting in three replicates of the four treatments. Initial height, root-collar diameter, and number of first-order lateral roots were recorded for each seedling. Seedlings were ocularly graded into one of two categories (premium and good) based on morphological characteristics. Outplantings were measured after the 2002 and 2003 growing season. Mean seedling survivorship after two growing seasons was 94, 92, 87 and 58 percent for the commercial clearcut, two-age, high-grade, and no-cut control units, respectively. Average growth of unbrowsed seedlings for the two growing seasons was 44 cm, 42 cm, 41 cm, 29 cm in the two-age, high-grade, commercial clearcut, and control treatments, respectively. Differences in seedling growth were found between the harvested units and control units ($P<0.005$) using Tukey-Kramer multiple comparisons. After two growing seasons, premium-graded seedlings grew an average 21 cm more than seedlings graded as good ($P<0.005$). In addition, seedlings browsed heavily by white-tail deer (*Odocoileus virginianus* (Boddaert)) during the 2002 and 2003 growing seasons were on average 36 cm ($P<0.001$) smaller than unbrowsed seedlings.

While differences in seedling growth within harvested units have not been documented after two growing seasons, high levels of mortality and diminished growth in the control units suggests that pre-harvest enrichment planting without competition control is not a viable management option. However, a simple ocular grading of seedlings prior to planting can result in significant growth gains early in the development of the seedlings.

NATURAL OAK REGENERATION 22 TO 35 YEARS AFTER CLEARCUTTING ON THE HOOSIER NATIONAL FOREST

Marcus F. Selig
Department of Forestry and Natural Resources, Purdue University
West Lafayette, IN 47907
John R. Seifert
Department of Forestry and Natural Resources, Purdue University, Southeast Purdue Agricultural Center,
Butlerville, IN 47223
and
Douglass F. Jacobs
Department of Forestry and Natural Resources, Purdue University
West Lafayette, IN 47907

Oak (*Quercus* spp.) recruitment failure is a severe problem in the Central Hardwood forest region. The majority of studies that have examined decreases in oak abundance were conducted over a relatively short time and across a very narrow landscape. This study examines oak regeneration by revisiting a number of former clearcut stands throughout the Hoosier National Forest in southern Indiana.

Seventy-four oak-dominated stands, of various sizes (2.8 to 23.1 hectares) and landscape attributes, were harvested between 1969 and 1982. The stands were measured in 1986 and 1987 and showed a marked decrease in natural oak regeneration. The stands are currently being reassessed over a three-year period to monitor the dynamics of harvested stands by comparing current results to pre-harvest stand composition and the results of the 1986-87 measurements. Sites are currently being sampled with approximately 2.5 plots per hectare. Each plot consists of a 0.04-hectare tree tally (>2.54 cm d.b.h.) and a 0.004-hectare reproduction plot (<2.54 cm d.b h.), similar to the previous measurement regime.

First-year results (20 stands sampled) indicate an increase in the dominant oak component since the 1986-1987 sampling, although oaks have yet to regain their former stand dominance. Prior to harvest, oaks comprised an average of 71 percent (38 trees per acre (TPA)) of the dominant trees in the sampled stands. During the 1986-1987 study, oaks represented only 8 percent (145 TPA) of the dominant trees, but now comprise an average of 20 percent (49 TPA) of the dominant trees in sampled stands.

A continued increase in the dominant oak component appears uncertain, as oaks comprise only 8 percent of intermediate and suppressed trees at this time. Preliminary results indicate that oaks may eventually regain dominant status; however, the time required for full oak representation may be greater than originally expected.

EFFECTS OF PERIODIC FIRE ON COMPOSITION AND LONG-TERM DYNAMICS OF ARKANSAS UPLAND HARDWOOD FORESTS

Martin A. Spetich
USDA Forest Service, Southern Research Station,
Arkansas Forestry Sciences Laboratory
Hot Springs, AR 71902

Prescribed fire (at historic periodic fire frequencies) is seen as an important but little understood tool in the assortment of management techniques that could help restore oak to Arkansas upland hardwood forests and facilitate the maintenance of these keystone species. However, no known periodic fire research has been done in Arkansas' unique upland hardwood forests. The objective of our study is to examine the effects of periodic fire on: (1) species dynamics, (2) renewal and survival of natural oak seedlings/saplings and planted oaks under varying overstory and understory treatments, (3) standing and down coarse woody debris, (4) fuel loading, (5) tree quality, (6) damage to residual trees, and (7) tree growth in fire versus non-fire areas.

Replications, each approximately 26 hectares in size, are now being installed in the Boston Mountains of northern Arkansas on three sites with medium and three sites with high site indices. Each replication is split so that half will receive periodic prescribed fire treatments and half will be protected from fire. There will be four overstory treatment and three understory treatment subplots within each main plot. Overstory treatments will consist of a shelterwood (40% stocking) harvest, 0.405 ha openings, improvement harvest (free thinning with a 16 m^2/ha target) and no harvest. Understory treatments have begun and consist of: (1) manual removal of the subcanopy (trees > 30 cm tall and up to 14 cm d.b h.) by manually cutting non-restoration tree species prior to prescribed fire, (2) cut surface herbicide treatment of the subcanopy (trees > 30 cm tall and up to 14 cm d.b h.) by treating non-restoration tree species prior to prescribed fire, and (3) no treatment of understory trees or shrubs. Two to three prescribed fires will be applied during the first 5 years after harvest and then at 4 year cycles for at least 4 cycles.

EARLY STAND DEVELOPMENT IN A RED OAK-PAPER BIRCH STAND REGENERATED THROUGH THE SHELTERWOOD SYSTEM IN NORTHERN WISCONSIN

Terry F. Strong
USDA Forest Service, North Central Research Station
Rhinelander, WI 54501

A study was established 20 years ago in northern Wisconsin to examine the minimum size of seedlings to ensure seedling survival after the overstory was removed in a red oak (*Quercus rubra* L.) and paper birch (*Betula papyrifera* Marsh.) stand. About 65 percent of the site was scarified in 1985 with a woods disc. The overstory was removed 3, 4, 5, and 6 years after scarification. The site index is poor for sugar maple (*Acer saccharum* Marsh.) (SI=50) but good for red oak and paper birch (SI=70 and 60, respectively).

Saplings were counted and measured 10 and 15 years after overstory removal. Red oak and paper birch success was highly dependent on scarification and amount of competition from shrubs (primarily raspberry). Red oak success was best in plots that were scarified and had little raspberry (*Rubus* spp.) competition. Red oak was the dominant sapling in 25 percent of these plots compared to only 11 percent in the unscarified plots. When raspberry was dominant, red oak seedlings survived that were 3 to 4 feet tall prior to overstory removal. When raspberry was not dominant, oak seedlings survived that were 2 feet tall prior to overstory removal. About 1,700 saplings/acre were present 15 years after overstory removal in the scarified plots with little raspberry present.

IMPACT OF ACORN MOISTURE CONTENT AT SOWING ON GERMINATION AND SEEDLING GROWTH OF WHITE OAK AND NORTHERN RED OAK

Shi-Jean Susana Sung and **Paul P. Kormanik**
USDA Forest Service, Southern Research Station
Athens, GA 30602
Taryn L. Kormanik
University of Georgia
Athens, GA 30602
and
Stanley J. Zarnoch
USDA Forest Service, Southern Research Station
Asheville, NC 28802

Acorn quality is an integral part of artificial oak regeneration. Progeny from individual mother trees of similar geographic areas frequently exhibited a wide range of germination percentage. The purpose of our study was to evaluate the impact of acorn moisture content (MC) at sowing on germination and subsequent seedling growth.

Acorns from ten mother trees each of white oak (*Quercus alba* L.) and northern red oak (*Q. rubra* L.) were collected locally and from south Georgia in October 2002. Mean acorn MC for white oak and northern red oak were 48 percent and 39 percent, respectively. Acorns were stored at 4° C until air dried on a laboratory bench in late November. White oak acorns were air dried for 2, 4, and 7 days to reach 40 percent, 30 percent, and 20 percent MC, respectively. Some white oak acorns had radicles protruding prior to air-drying treatments.

It took northern red oak about 1.5, 4.5, and 9 days of drying to reach 35 percent, 25 percent, and 15 percent acorn MC, respectively. All acorns were sown in early December. By early April, both species had finished germination. White oak acorns of 48 percent, 40 percent, 30 percent, and 20 percent MC had germination percentages of 70, 46, 12, and 1.4 percent, respectively. Except for the lowest MC level, northern red oak germination was not affected much by acorn MC at sowing. Acorns in the 40 percent, 35 percent, 25 percent, and 15 percent MC groups had germination percentages of 83, 79, 68, and 46 percent, respectively. In general MC at sowing had no affect on first year growth of either species if they germinated. Moreover, about 40 percent of northern red oak seedlings in each MC group met our outplanting criteria which are 70 cm height, 8 mm root collar diameter, and 5 first-order lateral roots for both oaks. Except for the lowest MC group, only 13 to 17 percent of white oak seedlings met the outplanting criteria.

A second white oak acorn MC study was implemented in fall 2003 and all acorns were sown before any radicle protrusion occurred. The treatments included air drying acorns to 33 and 25 percent MC and non-drying controls (48 percent MC). Before sowing, half of the acorns in each MC group were soaked in water for 48 hours to raise their MC to 46 to 50 percent. Germination percentages were 91, 48, and 19 percent for controls, 33 percent MC, and 25 percent MC, respectively. Soaking increased germination of 33 percent MC acorns to 70 percent and 25 percent MC acorns to 34 percent but did not affect the controls.

EVALUATING THE EFFECTIVENESS OF GROUND COVER MANAGEMENT IN OAK PLANTINGS AND STANDS

J. W. Van Sambeek
USDA Forest Service, North Central Research Station
Columbia, MO 65203-7260

Ground cover management in hardwood plantings will affect early survival and growth of hardwood seedlings. Although less frequently researched, the management of ground covers in hardwood plantings can also alter the growth of saplings and pole-sized hardwood trees. Although oaks (*Quercus* spp.) have been included in several replicated studies, it is difficult to determine the impacts on, or make recommendations among, the various practices. These practices can include managing the natural ground flora; controlling the competing vegetation using cultivation, chemicals, or mulching; underplanting with less competitive legumes or grasses; or interplanting with woody nurse crops. My proposed study will utilize existing published literature to determine the growth responses of oaks to ground cover treatments and compare these growth responses to other hardwood species.

Most replicated studies involving ground cover management in tree plantings include one of two controls - plots maintained free of competing vegetation by mechanical or chemical methods, or plots where the natural ground flora is allowed to develop. A database is currently being constructed from published literature that compares multi-year responses of hardwood seedlings, saplings, or pole-sized trees to various practices as a percentage of the response to one or both of these control treatments. This database currently contains information on tree species, study location, size class and specific experimental treatments, year established, initial and final tree size and age, and whether statistically significant differences were reported. The most significant problems encountered in creating the database have been unreported seedling sizes and control treatments that show negative or little growth during the reported test period.

Preliminary analyses indicate that oak seedling and sapling responses to ground cover management practices are similar to most other trees excluding short rotation, intensive culture hardwoods and conifers. Growth of oaks in either mowed plots or plots with unmanaged natural flora averages less than 45 percent of the growth reported for oaks in vegetation-free controls. Similar comparisons reveal growth reductions of 30 percent when oaks are underplanted with forage legumes or grasses. Organic mulches and nitrogen-based fertilizers on average increase oak growth by 20 to 30 percent over oaks in vegetation-free plots. Using results from other hardwood species and with the addition of more oak entries into the database from the existing literature, it may be possible to determine if species differences exist as to how competitive different forage legumes and grasses are likely to be on saplings and pole-sized oak trees.

EVALUATION OF ROOT FORCE™ CONTAINER SEEDLINGS OF FOUR OAK SPECIES FOR BOTTOMLAND FOREST RESTORATION IN SOUTHERN INDIANA: 2 YEAR RESULTS

Dale R. Weigel
USDA Forest Service, North Central Research Station
Bedford, IN 47421
and
Daniel C. Dey
USDA Forest Service, North Central Research Station
Columbia, MO 65211

Bottomland forest restoration has become an area of interest in the last 10 to 15 years due to large scale bottomland flooding. Seed sources for large heavy seeded species such as the various native bottomland oaks are nonexistent, thus planting seedlings is needed to increase the proportion of heavy seeded trees to diversify bottomland forests. Nursery-grown bareroot seedlings are not usually competitive and do not survive well in areas with heavy vegetation and grass, especially where herbicides cannot be used for competition control. Larger container-grown seedlings may be more competitive than bareroot seedlings in afforesting productive bottomlands.

We tested the field performance of one-year-old, large-rooted Root Force™ seedlings grown in 3.8- and 11.4-L containers and compared them with 1-0 bareroot seedlings at a bottomland restoration project along Otter Creek on the Hoosier National Forest in southern Indiana. Four bottomland oak species were used: bur (*Quercus macrocarpa* Michx.), pin (*Quercus palustris* Muenchh.), Shumard (*Quercus shumardii* Buckl.), and swamp white (*Quercus bicolor* Willd.). Seedlings were planted in a fescue-dominated bottomland pasture. Half of the seedlings had a weed control treatment that consisted of placing a 1.2- x 1.2-m weed barrier mat around each seedling. The remaining seedlings grew in direct competition with fescue grass and other vegetation.

Survival for all species and stock types was similar after the first-year, 99 to 100 percent, and second-year, 87 to 93 percent. Although the 3.8-L container-grown seedlings (shoot height, 30.9 cm, and diameter, 5.6 mm) were the smallest at planting, their survival after two years was highest. Survival for the 11.4-L container-grown seedlings was lowest even though their initial shoot diameter (7.8 mm) was larger than the 3.8-L container-grown seedlings. Shumard oak had the lowest survival rate after the second year. Weed control had no influence on survival either year.

For all four species, bareroot seedlings had the lowest net height growth after two years. The 11.4-L container-grown and bareroot seedlings showed negative height growth the second year. After two years, the 3.8-L container-grown seedlings remained the shortest in total height (initial height 30.9 cm) while the 11.4-L container-grown (initial height 51.6 cm) and bareroot seedlings (initial height 62.6 cm) were similar. In the 2 years, the 3.8-L container-grown seedlings grew 13 cm; the 11.4-L container-grown seedlings grew 6.5 cm, and the bareroot seedlings lost 3 cm in height. The height growth for all seedlings was influenced by deer browsing; thus there appeared to be no preference for any stock type. Two year field performance provides no clear superior stock type.

EFFECT OF STORAGE TEMPERATURE AND DURATION ON COLD HARDINESS AND DORMANCY OF NORTHERN RED OAK SEEDLINGS: USE OF THE ELECTROLYTE LEAKAGE PROCEDURE

Barrett C. Wilson and **Douglass F. Jacobs**
Hardwood Tree Improvement and Regeneration Center
Department of Forestry and Natural Resources, Purdue University
West Lafayette, IN 47907-2061

Electrolyte leakage (EL) has successfully predicted cold hardiness of conifer seedlings in both research and commercial settings. EL has also been performed experimentally on European hardwood species. The objective of our study was to determine if further refinement and adjustment of EL methodology to account for the unique characteristics of hardwood seedlings (e.g., seasonal loss of leaves) would result in a rapid, accurate approach to assessing cold hardiness, dormancy, and performance potential. In November 2002 we initiated a study to evaluate the effect of storage regime on changes in cold hardiness and dormancy of seedlings of several hardwood species. The impact of cold storage and freezer storage on the physiological status of northern red oak (*Quercus rubra* L.) was assessed at durations of 2, 3, 4, and 5 months.

To get an estimation of the depth of dormancy, seedlings were removed from storage and grown in a greenhouse to monitor the number of days to budbreak (DBB). To evaluate changes in freezing tolerance, the EL procedure was employed. Stem samples were collected from seedlings and subjected to controlled freeze tests at 4, -10, -20, and -40° C. Tissue damage at each temperature was expressed as a percentage of the initial EL values to those after autoclaving.

Results indicated that DBB decreased as storage duration increased, ranging from 42 to 45 days after 2 months of storage to 12 to 20 days after 5 months of storage. After 5 months of storage, freezer-stored seedlings required more DBB than cold-stored seedlings. We found significant freeze test and storage duration main effects for EL values. Tissue damage increased with lower freezing temperatures and extended storage durations. In addition, a freeze test x duration interaction was present when EL increased at lower freeze test temperatures after 3, 4, and 5 months, but not after 2 months of storage. Freezer-stored seedlings tended to have the greatest EL, but this was not consistent. Simple linear regression analysis showed EL values at -20° C and -40° C to be good indicators of dormancy status. Though these results are promising, more intensive study is needed to assess the viability of EL in predicting of dormancy and hardiness for hardwood species across a variety of environmental conditions.

RESPONSE OF OUTPLANTED NORTHERN RED OAK SEEDLINGS UNDER TWO SILVICULTURAL PRESCRIPTIONS IN NORTH ALABAMA

Callie Jo Schweitzer
USDA Forest Service, Southern Research Station
Normal, Alabama 35762
Emile Gardiner
USDA Forest Service, Southern Research Station
Center for Bottomland Hardwood Research
Stoneville, Mississippi 38776
and
Stephanie Love and **Tom Green**
Alabama A&M University
Normal, Alabama 35762

The decision to artificially regenerate oak must be predicated on some basis. After completing an assessment of the potential to regenerate oak naturally, we decided our stands might benefit from supplemental oak plantings. The primary objective of this study was to couple outplanting of northern red oak (*Quercus rubra* L.) with applied silviculture prescriptions in north Alabama. Outplanting light conditions were quantified and seedling survival, growth, and photosynthetic light response curves were developed.

In 2002, northern red oak seedlings were grown from acorns under full ambient (sun) and half-ambient (shade) light conditions in a greenhouse. Seedlings grown under full sun conditions were significantly taller, had more leaves, and more flushes per seedling compared to those seedlings grown in shade. There was no significant difference in root collar diameter. Seedlings were hand-planted in the field in February of 2003. Seedlings from each greenhouse light condition were planted either in a clearcut or under an oak shelterwood.

There were three replicates of each outplanted stand. The oak shelterwood was created in November 2002 by using an herbicide to selectively remove mid-canopy species; no gaps were created in the overstory canopy. The clearcut was harvested in winter 2002. The clearcut had 5 ft^2/acre residual basal area, 32 percent canopy cover, and 69 percent of photosynthetic active radiation (PAR) compared to above canopy levels. Residual basal area for the oak shelterwood was 70 ft^2/acre, 98 percent canopy cover, and 14 percent of PAR compared to above canopy levels. Competition was mechanically controlled and the outplanting sites were fenced.

Survival was high for all outplanted seedlings. Seedlings grown under full ambient light (sun seedlings) and outplanted in the clearcut had greater basal diameter growth than both sun and shade seedlings outplanted in the shelterwood. Previous exposure to higher ambient light levels (sun seedlings) did not result in greater light use for outplanted seedlings the following growing season. Outplanting light conditions affected physiological response, as net photosynthetic rate was greater for seedlings outplanted in clearcut compared to shelterwood conditions. Light saturation and light compensation point were significantly less for shelterwood seedlings compared to those in clearcut. Ambient light intensity (125 umol/m^2/s) under the shelterwood was, on average, below the light saturation level (151 umol/m^2/s).

UPLAND HARDWOOD RESEARCH IN ARKANSAS BOSTON MOUNTAINS - AN INTEGRATED APPROACH

Martin A. Spetich
USDA Forest Service, Southern Research Station
Arkansas Forestry Sciences Laboratory
Hot Springs, AR 71902

This integrated research program addresses upland hardwood forest dynamics and the development of both short and long-term studies at three scales: individual tree, stand, and region. These studies address: growth, woody species reproduction, competitive capacity, stand dynamics, stand composition, forest species restoration, quantitative silviculture, development of forest management methods, forest ecology, disturbance ecology, and diversity of upland hardwood forests of Arkansas Interior Highlands. Information already produced from these studies include publications and products addressing oak decline; land use history; fire ecology; and regional dynamics of upland old-growth forests of the Midwest; and an interactive web-based product based on this research (see http://ncrs.fs fed.us/oakus/).

HARVEST SURVIVABILITY OF OAK ADVANCED REGENERATION

Jeff Stringer
Department of Forestry, University of Kentucky
Lexington, KY 40546-0073

Natural regeneration of oak requires the occurrence of advance regeneration and/or stems capable of stump sprouting. These stems must be present before harvest and adequate numbers must survive harvest for oaks to successfully regenerate. Regeneration predictions are based on pre-harvest advance regeneration inventories. However, the use of these inventories does not account for losses that can occur to the advance regeneration pool during harvest operations. This research was designed to determine the survivability of oak advance regeneration subjected to a ground skidding harvest associated with commercial clearcutting.

This study assessed the harvest survivability of advance regeneration of a number of species in four mixed species upland oak stands in Kentucky. Seven regeneration plots were established using a systematic random grid on each of four 8-acre harvest areas. One regeneration plot was centrally located in each of the seven sections. The regeneration plots included one 0.01-acre fixed area plot (28 total) and three 0.001-acre plots (84 total). All trees > 4.5 ft tall to 10 inches diameter-at-breast-height in the larger plot and all stems 0.5 to 4.5 ft tall in the mil acre plots were permanently located with a combination tag composed of a heavy aluminum number tag and a whisker tag pinned to the ground with #9 galvanized wire. Species, height, and groundline diameter were measured prior to harvest. Directly after harvest each tag was located and the stem was coded as either present or absent. Each tree was placed into a height class and a groundline diameter class for analysis. Regression was used to determine relationships between survival (dependent variable) and groundline diameter and height (independent variables).

Each area was subjected to a fall harvest, completed with manual felling and ground skidding. All merchantable stems greater than 8 inches in diameter were removed. Slopes averaged approximately 20 percent and wheeled skidders were able to run unimpeded throughout the tracts. Percent survival varied by height, groundline diameter, and species. Analysis by height classes across all species found that survival was different between stems taller than and shorter than 3.0 ft in height. Oaks < 3 ft in height averaged 55.3 percent survival while those > 3 ft in height averaged 90.2 percent survival. The relationship between total height and survival for all species yielded the best fit simple linear regression ($y=0.7187+0.0924*x$, $r^2 = 0.66$) and the best fit linear regression ($1/y=0.0167+(-0.0032)*\ln(x)$, $r^2 = 0.87$). As would be expected analysis of survival by groundline diameter classes mirrored the results of the analysis by height. The relationship between survival and groundline diameter yielded the best fit regression ($\ln y=0.1613+(-0.2534)/x^{0.5}$, $r^2=0.80$).

The outcomes of this study allow regeneration models to be adjusted for harvest mortality. Further analysis of data from this study will provide logistic regressions for individual oak species as well as other important competing species (ex. red maple (*Acer rubrum* L.)) on medium quality sites.

INDEX TO OAK (*QUERCUS*) SPECIES INCLUDED IN ONE OR MORE ABSTRACTS

Sub genus and species[1]	Common Name	Pages
RED OR BLACK OAK GROUP (SECTION *LOBATAE*)		
Q. agrifolia Nee	Coast live oak	13
Q. kelloggii Newb.	California black oak	13
Q. nigra L.	Water oak	1, 11
Q. nuttalli Palmer	Nuttall oak	11
Q. pagoda Raf. .	Cherrybark oak	1, 10
Q. palustris Muenchh.	Pin oak	3, 9, 22
Q. parvula v. shrevei	Shreve oak	13
Q. phellos L.	Willow oak	1, 11
Q. rubra L.	Northern red oak	2, 5, 6, 8, 15, 16, 19, 20, 23, 24
Q. shumardii Buckl.	Shumard oak	22
Q. veluntina Lam.	Black oak	4
WHITE OAK GROUP (SECTION *QUERCUS*)		
Q. alba L.	White oak	4, 14, 20
Q. bicolor Willd.	Swamp white oak	3, 22
Q. macrocarpa Michx.	Bur oak	22
INTERMEDIATE OAK GROUP (SECTION *PROTOBALANUS*)		
Q. chrysolepis Liebm.	Canyon live oak	13

[1]Fralish, James S; Franklin, Scott B. 2002. Taxonomy and Ecology of Woody Plants in North American Forests. New York, NY: John Wiley & Sons, Inc. 612 p.

U.S. Department of Agriculture, Forest Service.
  2005. Weigel, D.R.; Van Sambeek, J.W.; Michler, C.H., eds. **Ninth workshop on seedling physiology and growth problems in oak plantings (abstracts)**; 2004 October 18-20; West Lafayette, IN. Gen. Tech. Rep. NC-262. St. Paul, MN: U.S. Department of Agriculture, Forest Service, North Central Research Station. 28 p.

  Research results and ongoing research activities in field performance of oak plantings, seedling propagation, genetics, acorn germination, and natural regeneration of oaks are described in 26 abstracts.

  KEY WORDS: Plantations, propagation, regeneration.

www.ingramcontent.com/pod-product-compliance
Lightning Source LLC
Chambersburg PA
CBHW080739290526
45790CB00008B/3251